BY A THREAD

by Karen Kellock Ph.D.

Manual for
Superior Men

A complete theory based on Einstein physics,
Political Psychology, Systems Theory
and Archetypal Psychiatry.

FORMULA

All success attraction
All disease obstruction
All recovery elimination

You must fast on all three

OBSTRUCTIONS:

People
Habit
Food

BY A THREAD

Do not rely on people. it's great when encouraging but what happens when they flake out? Adversity builds these instincts and whether social muscle or brain power, hard circumstances creates genius. Stronger, more capable of handling extreme upsets, surviving what comes at them: these are the champions. Promotion does not come from people, it comes from the Lord--this releases the need to suckup to the mob for the less you depend on people the more you co-create with God.

BY A THREAD

HE HAS THE TABLE ALREADY PREPARED

RECOGNIZING DISRESPECT
QUEEN CONSCIOUSNESS
YOUR WORK IS YOUR IDENTITY
PESTERING
SEX ED NOT MATH OR HISTORY
THE MEAN SELFISH SOCIAL
UNSWERVINGLY PURE
A DUMBED DOWN GENERATION
DADS TEACH YOUR DAUGHTERS
FEAR OF HUMAN MEANNESS
BROKEN CONSCIOUSNESS
OVER-GRATITUDE TO THE RUDE
GOD GIVES IDENTITY NOT MAN
SAD LACK OF IDENTITY IN WOMEN
THE PUT-DOWN IS NONVERBAL
PEOPLE ARE CRUEL
FOR VICTORY DEFINE THE ENEMY
DISRESPECT IS DANGEROUS
HATERS GOTTA HATE
QUEEN CONSCIOUSNESS
DON'T HAVE TO SELL QUALITY
THEY LOVE YOU THEN HATE YOU
HE TOOK ADVANTAGE OF YOUR DAMAGE
ACCUSTOMED TO DISRESPECT
YOU DROPPED THE BAR SO LOW
LEARN TO LOVE STABILITY ONLY
TREACHERY OF THE LOVELY
BACKSTABBING SLANDERERS
DISHONOR FROM MEN

BY A THREAD

HE HAS THE TABLE ALREADY PREPARED

BY A THREAD
HE HAS THE TABLE ALREADY PREPARED

ADAPTANTS IN YOUR HOME
TRAUMA = FATAL MENTAL ILLNESS
NO NURTURANCE FROM OLD REJECTORS
HE HAS THE TABLE ALREADY PREPARED
BULIMIA IS A LETHAL MENTAL ILLNESS
LOW SELF-WORTH STARTS IN INFANCY
ALCOHOLIC ANOREXIA
HATRED OF SOCIAL OCCASIONS
SOCIAL CIRCUITRY VS. RECLUSIVITY
THOUGHT-SUBSTITUTION
ANOSOGNOSIA IS LETHAL
MENTAL ILLNESS BY OTHER PEOPLE
MARRIAGE IS A BEAUTIFUL WALL
EMBARRASSMENT/SHAME ACCEPTANCE
HANGING ON TO PAST PEOPLE
NO PAST EQUALS WORLD RENOWNED
THE WORLD HATES THE DEVIL IN YOU
STOP SAYING "UNITY" IS THE WAY
RECOGNIZE SINS OF DETRACTORS
ALL OF LIFE IMPOSED ON
SHAME FOR LETTING EM IN
BEING ALONE IS HIDEOUS TO THEM
ANTI-WHITE RACISM
HAD TO PLAY THEIR GAME
FEMINISTS GANG UP ON THE RECLUSE
SHOOOTING AT SHADOWS
PROMOTION NOT FROM PEOPLE
THE IMPOSSIBLE DREAM IS ALREADY HERE
THEY ARE IRRELEVANT NOW—LET EM GO

BY A THREAD

HE HAS THE TABLE ALREADY PREPARED

SEE THE SYSTEM THEN LET IT GO
PRISON PREPARATION THEN ERASE EM
KIDS ARE DEMONS WITHOUT LIMITS
THANK YOU FOR WHAT YOU'VE ALREADY DONE
SUDDENLY A GREAT CONTACT
YOU WEREN'T SUPPOSED TO GET IT
SEE THE ROT OR PART OF IT
NO ONE COULD EVER IMAGINE
WRITING IS ABOUT COPY NOT ME
ALL FAMILIES HAVE AN ODD PERSON OUT
SOCIAL PSYCHOLOGY: THE HERD
SIN CONTAINS IT'S OWN CONSEQUENCES
LIBERALISM IS A POWERFUL RELIGION
FLAT NON-DYNAMIC PERSONALITIES
ELITE COMMUNICATION IS SUBTLE
THEY CONSTRUCT MYTHICAL WORLDS
THE GREAT WORK IS COMPLETE BUT GOTTA WAIT
PEOPLE-WORSHIP IS PURE IDOLATRY
SOCIAL CHANGE WITH DEMOGRAPHIC SHIFTS
MEDIA IS THE DEMOCRATIC PARTY
KEYWORDS ARE VERY TELLING
MEN KISSING MEN, WOMEN KISSING WOMEN
DIET UPDATES
SMOOTHIES, SOUPS, STEWS
RECAP ON THEIR EVIL MAP
RECAP OF THE CREATIVE ACT
THE TRADITIONS OF MEN VS. GOD
LIES WE BUY/WHAT TO BUY

BY A THREAD

If you're playing out a false self you're hanging by a thread. Cuz you're a live wire, or dead.

Who can determine your value but your Creator? Yet you let em define you with their words.

RECOGNIZING DISRESPECT

Recognizing and confronting disrespect when it's subtle and non-verbal is for you, essential.

The put-down is nonverbal, don't forget that now. You sense it deeply and it hurts like hell.

You've been put down, disrespected and hate being snubbed. Now you're ready to love.

You know you're on the right path if a drive to do something without caring what they think.

If you wanna make it before you die the answer is HABITS to develop a porcelain finish.

You've already done all the work so now the whole Creative Act just goes on auto-pilot.

You've got the best habits: arising at midnight, eating one meal a day, staying in isolation.

Prosperity is the result of habits, period. Anything can be overcome by setting your mind to it.

QUEEN CONSCIOUSNESS

The Queen or King Consciousness is what everyone's designed for: it's called Dominion.

BY A THREAD

The downward spiral of women from queen consciousness is sickening/accelerating.

There's a strain of women-hating today that's unseen before now when patriarchy was the way.

The way you let em toy with you like a puppet while settling for nothing, you must now stop it.

It seems like a peaceful street but get involved with any one of em, meet conceit/take a backseat.

There's a strain of women-hate unseen in patriarchy where there's at least respect for the weak.

We become so broken adapting to other people we're out of sync with self, goals on the shelf.

She divorced herself from her own dignity, begging people to stay with one so dull/silly.

YOUR WORK IS YOUR IDENTITY

Do your work to gain identity instead of scrounging around and hanging on for dear life.

She's searching for identity cuz the world always lies about who you are, especially women see.

Around dummies you adapt to a very low life level and life becomes dull--that about says it all.

When they try to count us out/hold us back we just apply more pressure: Trump's our exemplar.

There's a strain of female-hate if they dare deviate and every herd has it's limits triggering hate.

As addictions are coping mechanisms to deal with bad feelings , they get worse naturally.

13

BY A THREAD

The dry years are part of a Hero's Path. Inside it's fertile anarchy yet it seems nothing's happening.

I let go of human society and explored the absolute: just God and I with many little animals too.

These were the best years of my life: alone, in the wilderness, in a tiny cabin with a bike.

They haven't done a thing. It's all embarrassing self-promotion built on a string and boring.

PESTERING

Before feminism women felt "pestered" by their husbands, not being as sexual like them.

"Pestering"—a common word back then--referred to the constant male drive to mate with them.

Feminism told women they had the same drive as men and thus they became promiscuous, amen.

Tho' content as single I didn't know what I was missing in a true home protected from evil.

Stop pestering. me, let me do my work! No I don't wanna thrash around in bed you jerk.

I once knew a town slut who had every man under her thumb, saying she slept with all of em.

They were also her flying monkeys, so if she's mad [or jealous] of you they attack you angrily.

She bragged about giving "BJs" so naturally the wives were this floozie's natural enemies.

Every town has one. She has maximum power over men but spiritually powerless, amen.

BY A THREAD

Talking about sex so much makes it as common as going to the bathroom--its ridiculous.

Women are even chasing men now. Females should never chase a man, it goes against God.

Kids go crazy/commit suicide having sex so early, without understanding, meaninglessly.

One mate after another, serial broken relationships, valueless, amoral brainwashed idiots.

SEX ED NOT MATH OR HISTORY

Education was sexualized in the 70's when everyone was doing it and it was rewarded as OK.

Not math/history/science but SEX was it. Making us immoral gave globalists control, get it?

They want us ruined from sex perversions so they can control us from the predictable outcome.

From my trumpet teacher at twelve to my Ph.D. sponsor at 26 they all tried to molest me.

I thought old men were nice. More often they're not, having become obdurate in sin and vice.

By midlife we're all a haunted house inside, from our own sins and the drastic cultural slide.

The most popular soaps are all on adultery and secret office romances of the ungodly.

Women LOVE this stuff, our main interest is relationships, even getting a Ph.D. in it.

Instead of hankering for affairs women should be focusing on their own homes I declare.

To repeat: If they can make us immoral they can control us, and it all starts with the kids.

It's not an outer but an **INNER** journey of enlightenment but most are derailed/prevented from this.

THE MEAN SELFISH SOCIAL

The SEX ED schools stress SOCIAL the most and that is what derails us from our real growth.

They want us SOCIAL not just sexed, it means conformity and for globalism that's the gist.

A hedonistic culture is a mean/selfish one where fidelity & trust is rare/kids go wrong sooner.

The kids I met in '85 were mean, selfish, brutal, violent, sensuous and totally self-indulgent.

Maturity or the ability to postpone gratification for a long range goal was now a lost value.

Their growth was derailed by the sexual and that was the plan all the time, to keep us dumbed.

They didn't care if I was good in math and science, not having social skills I didn't have a chance.

No wasted time on social skills in fact I resented peers--even as a youngster I sought the inner.

It's a terrifying atmosphere expected to be social when you have no desire to do so/be so loco.

Young girls have no trained defenses against the constant male sex drive in fact it's denied.

It's just constant sex: plumbing. When it's just plumbing how is life meaningful honey?

UNSWERVINGLY PURE

BY A THREAD

You must be unswervingly pure. It's a yes or no, never a lukewarm, it's a binary for sure.

Do you feel lost like a stranger in a strange land? I felt this way since I started Kindergarten.

A DUMBED DOWN GENERATION

If you can get along with a dumbed down generation then what's it say about you? Low IQ.

Europe: I love the scenery & history but not the wine {I don't drink] nor the kissing & hugging.

There were problems with patriarchy but men had much more respect for the ladies I'll say.

Who wouldn't appreciate their gallantry living in this world of misogyny—I recall the treachery.

A dumbed down generation is slow and clueless, soon everyone seems like soyboys/beta males.

Most women have been molested cuz people are rapacious esp. in a land without morals.

Pudgy upper arms, man boobs, big but and thighs, gut/uncut, nice but it's all by rote/duds.

Men of past were all there—totally present and engaging—but then things were civil.

It's even become a fad to leave women off in other cities, vulnerable to terrible tragedies.

He kindly invited her to live in, she burned her bridges and he proceeded to torture the woman.

DADS TEACH YOUR DAUGHTERS

BY A THREAD

Dads teach daughters to guard their goods cuz they're meant for divinity where queens stood.

We're MEANT to take dominion--that's a king or queen--but this conscious is broken.

Mom started getting nervous around holidays cuz a genius hates the twits/time commitments.

Fear of being ridiculed, attacked or mocked can push one into isolation which is ultimately good.

There are female geniuses and they go crazy if not firmly harnessed in God, hopefully.

Exposure may mean being mocked, ridiculed and even attacked so be careful there honey.

FEAR OF HUMAN MEANNESS

Fear of human meanness ruled my life. A stranger in a strange land where NO ONE seems nice.

It's when the cruelty of men makes her run to another man for protection in pure repetition.

It's like God gave me one escape hatch after another, appearing at the last moment as savior.

I still fear em coming around the corner: the Jezebels and wicked men I've known on the earth.

I barely escaped em then God took em out. I swear, the end's not good for haters of God.

It's the wicked who collude together on bringing down the king/queen and it's pure envy.

In my home behind a locked gate I can be happy every day cuz I'm not influenced by the fray.

BY A THREAD

Sudden flashbacks, lucid recall, gems remind "I won't do that again". But PTSD is constant.

BROKEN CONSCIOUSNESS

When queen consciousness becomes broken she does not know who she is so settles for less.

As a naive girl she burned her bridges and moved in with him. At his mercy she met her end.

At this time most women have not had fathers to inform them and teach em protection.

No one told me men would want a piece of me then reject me, no one warned about envy.

No one coached me on how to push back against men touching me-- molestation being key.

I had to learn everything the hard way. It's a ruthless and dirty world: warn your daughters ok.

I can't believe what I put up with, let pass by, ignored or just hoped would soon go away.

The casual attitude towards sex is sickening to one with queen consciousness, it's hellish.

The idea of personal boundaries was unknown to me. I was an open book but isolation saved me.

Boundaries are ALL: Because they're either putting their hands on you or talking about it doll.

Personal Boundaries Marks the Queen: It's No, No, No, No, No! And never stop saying it: NO.

But the girls today don't/can't say NO. In giving in they are the losers forever in a lion's den.

Sex is an invasion of privacy, boundaries and an implanting of spirits from their histories.

With illicit sex he's the victor & you're the loser girl, left to fend for yourself in this evil world.

OVER-GRATITUDE TO THE RUDE

Due to prior mistreatment I was over-grateful he opened my door/said pleased to meet you.

The mission of queenology is to make all women conscious of how they're made see.

You hate men invading your space cuz inside you're a queen--but docile, you lose your sheen.

With blocked energy [not objecting] your queenly illumination darkens [aura is muddy].

Lost identity darkens the mind/stops the creative spark and it happens with just one remark.

First tenet of Queenology: self-awareness [identity] is our relationship with God & unique gifts.

The second tenet is Self-Mastery. Self-discipline and repentance of sins makes a true lady.

Self-sufficiency means INDEPENDENCE. The lady is motivated to trust God not beg inferiors.

The queen trusts God for necessities and never pleads/begs inferiors to take care of her.

Queenly self-projection [confidence]. Never invisible in any space because she has presence.

A queen makes a statement without saying a word. Assertion when necessary but no slurs.

BY A THREAD

Tho' assertive at times the queen leaves her mark with grace, humility, excellence and kindness.

Self-Actualization/manifestation: Not wasting potential on secondary matters but a vision.

A queen avoids useless tangents: every vision, dream and assignment will thus be manifested.

GOD GIVES IDENTITY NOT MAN

I will live my life as the complete expression of who I was created to be, more every day. Lady

What is Queen Consciousness? Knowing who you are from soul and spirit. It's cute/it's you sis.

It's the self-concept you have etched into your subconscious, a template of you sis.

Queens know who they are in their spirit. They don't need nor do they welcome outside input.

I know who I am/don't need a world to tell me who I am: after a life of hard knocks this happened.

She kept telling me how good I looked and I found it irritating--how most females are stuck.

The queen can introduce herself to the world because she knows who she is from her soul.

She is thus defined by her internal faculties as opposed to the world around her see.

My broken consciousness sent me alone to the desert wilderness to rebuild Her Highness.

I had evil spirits from my male persecutors/the female hawks and had to spiritually detox

21

BY A THREAD

Queens know our internal faculties defines you, not the world around which MISDEFINES you.

I was so broken I couldn't get up. All from being a victim/not knowing how to make it stop.

SAD LACK OF IDENTITY IN WOMEN

Most women are so sadly lacking in definition they're in a panic begging chumps to define them.

She feels like she needs something other that self and God to BE. It's torture feeling empty.

She wants a man, a baby, her closet's full of clothes with tags still on em--all striving for identity.

It was either produce or be seen as crazy. Having something to show changed image suddenly.

It's ever-searching for something vs. knowing who you are from your very soul needing nothing.

When broken she settles for any man to bring her definition/wants a baby for the same reason.

When broken there's nothing outside that can fix it. Go back to God not outer sources/lunatics.

She even tries to increase her status position by having sex with one not her husband.

Later she realizes fulfillment only comes from God inside and the Self He made bonafide.

After wasting time giving herself to bums who didn't deserve her she awakes to self-sufficiency.

Some have been misdefined all their life--not wonderfully and marvelously made, aye.

BY A THREAD

In the emotions there's a confirmation of Who I Am in the Creator's eyes: that's the high prize.

Most women can't find the Creator's definition cuz they're constantly looking outward in sum.

THE PUT-DOWN IS NONVERBAL

85% of all communication is non-verbal. Stop hearing words and look at the signs from hell.

Nonverbal messages: Ignoring, walking by without acknowledging and this is repeated often.

When it comes to communication [what they're truly saying] listen to your gut--is this a SHUN?

Who cares what he thinks? It's what the bible says not his silly thoughts, he's a narcissist!

I totally related to her: Blanche in Streetcar, a hyper-sensitive tormented by a bear.

They justified his sin cuz he's a cousin. That's the evil of nepotism versus good judgment.

They were like ravenous wolves when I moved into the neighborhood and it was pure hatred.

PEOPLE ARE CRUEL

People are cruel. Dis-acknowledging someone publicly is one nonverbal message among many.

Don't get so involved with your neighbors. Just cuza propinquity you put up with losers?

He was obviously--in my face see--dis-acknowledging me and I recognized it as messaging.

For all behavior is communicational and a healthy minded person instantly recognizes it all.

Here I am enjoying the scenery and suddenly I'm embroiled in someone's insanity.

This is the way it always is whenever involved with humans and MOST are narcissists.

There's no enjoying the scenery when living around humans and their petty jealousies.

The more you give them [to stave em off] the more they hate you, that's the multitudes.

FOR VICTORY DEFINE THE ENEMY

They hate me for my work. It's different from what they think, that's all it takes at first.

For victory all it takes is Define your Enemy. Then a solution rolls out and you're on your way.

If you live around humans don't get so involved with the scenery you forget the enemy.

Your lovely country neighborhood's about to be absorbed up into a global cog Bud.

Turn off the news to avoid the constant repeats of how they're lying to us cuz we know this.

The narcissist accuses then cultural prejudices enter in and they've got you, a scapegoat shoe in.

Get control of your mind. Your enemies are dead or gone, made of none effect or dumbed.

Less. cops, more crooks, less consequences--but that results in more guns per residences.

BY A THREAD

Marching for causes they don't understand based on unproven arguments/destructive fear.

Selfish, badly educated virtue-signaling asses craving luxury and the feeling of noble causes.

Living in a ghost town on 1000 acres for 26 years I conquered loneliness and all my fears.

DISRESPECT IS DANGEROUS

You left me in other cities, there's no telling what you'd do next so I escaped/you called it crazy.

There's no way I'd ever get in a car with you again let alone trust you in any way for a living.

So the opinion leader of the tribe puts you down then they all call you a clown: the dumbed.

If you don't like the music, words, theory or therapy picturestrips then don't go there.

Seeing the ugly side of human nature cuz you're on the downside can change you for sure.

To learn how to lead go to jail or try to adapt to the old bitty, the crone or the moody whale.

First they admire you then one says you're nothing then they all hate you for fooling them.

I was angry like anyone caught in a contradiction but I wrote it all down while laying in the sun.

Who'd wanna be younger and go through those lessons again--recall the torture of adapting.

Holocaust comparisons are deliberately exploiting the murder of 6 million for their own positions.

Gossiping: Something setting them apart for persecution, making them a target of anyone.

The evils of nepotism: He stole $4000 worth of materials but it was denied by his cousin.

Success doesn't come from east or west but God who puts one up as He puts another down.

HATERS GOTTA HATE

He doesn't have to go to my page but is bothered anyway. He doesn't want me to exist see.

More [words] is not more, only less is more and that's the value of verse: most memorizable.

He was a boy with no limits/I was scared to death by his presence but I still was a good hostess.

Despite him being a lecher, scammer, liar and thief they believed the Old Man not me.

It seems peaceful on the surface but get involved with these people, it's a rabbit hole of evil.

nstead of self-promotion give just a tiny paragraph on you: Like St. Theresa said, go small.

You either handle me as a priority or an object of disrespect. It's queen consciousness.

There's nothing consistent about a double-minded man. He wants this but then wants that.

QUEEN CONSCIOUSNESS

Being a queen-conscious woman there should be a distinction about you vs. the crowd.

BY A THREAD

A queen is designed to stand out and even be alone if she has to--that means never to settle.

You're not a weak little woman who needs attachment for identity purposes--it's protection sis.

Gossipings, rumblings, rumors, dyads, triads and jealousy triangles: that's the system.

She tells you the bad things her family and friends said about you and you said Go To Hell.

She liked you at first but then spoke to the others and came back giving the cold shoulder.

You don't see Rolls Royce commercials for the quality of the car is so obviously impeccable.

DON'T HAVE TO SELL QUALITY

You don't have to sell it, its quality speaks for it. Don't self-promote just do your work, devote.

A queen isn't upset they all aren't hollering at her, she's not a chevy she's a Rolls Royce dear.

Her impeccable quality goes with no-compromise policy: blending in disguises value see.

Never compromise or drop your standards due to age. There's a panic and pressures degrade.

Compromise damages the brain and psyche: a broken mindset of self-respect or paradigm.

You're not on someone else's time table. Whether you're 20 or seventy it's your unique destiny.

The liberal will strip you of your godly identity and destiny--if weak you'll cave in totally.

BY A THREAD

I hate you milking the archetype of the sultan or dirty old man when you've got nothing.

Compromise damages the brain and psyche: a broken paradigm or self-respect mindset.

Everyone hates her/feels sorry for him being married to a savage like the wife of the alcoholic.

He's a social manipulator and she's a hypersensitive being constantly wounded/blamed for it.

No one could believe he was the culprit behind the scenes, triggering her to wild displays.

THEY LOVE YOU THEN HATE YOU

First they think you're great but then a spirit of familiarity arises and you're low rate.

"I suffered for years as a wife of a dam alcoholic and I'll never be one again." Lady survivor

He knew just how to trigger her so he'd always come out the victim and her the evil harridan.

Subconsciously you keep thinking "I'm just an option" no matter what you wanna call it hon'.

"I may as well settle, I'm just an option". But God says be not conformed/renew your mind son.

The recluse gets so crazy she makes a wild social display then is remembered that way.

With compromise you damage your psyche and begin to believe inferiors are actually superior.

You damage your psyche by dropping your standards until you even start look up to libtards.

BY A THREAD

Every time one settles to compromise they damage their psyche and look UP to creepy guys.

"I know he won't be faithful but I'll be alright"--a damaged psych living with a narcissist.

HE TOOK ADVANTAGE OF YOUR DAMAGE

The narcissist will always take advantage of your damage and then the pain excruciates.

With a damaged psych from him/her, waiting for honor becomes your dysfunctional norm.

The damaged victim rejects the notion that being their PRIORITY could even be a possibility.

He's so slow you knew what he was gonna say twenty minutes ago: a speedbump you know.

His postorgasmic emotional withdrawal triggers her early trauma of abandonment that's all.

It's the emotional level that keeps a poet's words flowing and they're as deep as the ocean.

The blocked energy landed on the drive which was a palliative and she was blinded by it.

We've been around, we sense things deeply. If there's disrespect it breaks down our psyche.

ACCUSTOMED TO DISRESPECT

I would never want to be younger because of what I had to go through to get exactly here.

She got it all twisted up so much she could not believe she could ever be a man's priority.

BY A THREAD

You've gotten so broken you're no longer offended by disrespect--here's where it gets bad.

No longer offended at BLATANT disrespect they can cuss you out and you just stay numb.

I don't like being snubbed. It's a coward's way of saying F-U without facing/working it out.

Recognize the nonverbal signs of disrespect or stay twisted in the wind in painful neglect.

The husband is cuckolded when his wife is obviously disrespected and he just ignores it.

She begins to over-value basic respect as extraordinary, thrown crumbs/being sorry.

YOU DROPPED THE BAR SO LOW

She dropped the bar so low that any man could come in with the basics like please/thank you.

He says "hello ma'am" and she inflates him to a saint's status of respect for lowly scum.

She's overwhelmed with admiration for a saint just cuz he opened her door without complaints.

It's a generation of women who've been so mistreated just basic respect makes him a saint.

Growing hatred of women: he left me off to hitchhike home, he shut my housecat out to roam.

I became so over-grateful it was shameful. I couldn't believe he gave me respect tho' minimal.

It's common: He gave me so much respect I thought there was something wrong with him.

BY A THREAD

I had gotten so used to the low bar of respect I expected neglect and more emptiness.

She wants the man who runs mind games on her and sabotage a great situation for a future.

Broken consciousness says: "He respects and provides for me but I'm not attracted really".

Millions of women would love to have your man and your life but you want the flashy guy.

LEARN TO LOVE STABILITY ONLY

Learn to love home STABILITY which allows you to expand utility and love develops see.

Watch the archetypes that a man plays out. Is it of a sultan with young women all around?

If a woman puts up with these things she's got personal work to do--delay relationship.

Solution: You need a relationship with Creator and yourself or continue being dogged out.

Continue being an option and your psyche will just get more broken, broken and broken.

You must pause this thing. Heal, learn, self-correct and truly understand what is respect.

Learn the ropes so you're no longer vulnerable to men with silver tongues or chug-a-lugs.

A woman with self-respect will instantly walk away and never look back, that's like our first lady.

Making you blue: Getting in your head, saying all that stuff so you start doubting your value.

TREACHERY OF THE LOVELY

Genius in a liberal environment is bashed and muted and the whole tribe is thus polluted.

Inconvenient/genius women are slandered by liberals constantly and it's usually false see.

If you always feel hurt you wouldn't be if you read Psalms everyday re: common treachery.

The Kings of the earth gather to pull you down but God knowing their end laughs at the clowns.

It may help you to expect it rather than always feeling dejected--it's a sign of your greatness.

The liberal losers in the family will pin the most horrible and despicable labels on the gentle.

They will slander them with the crimes which they do, it's always that way-- remember that too.

To be slandered your whole life sux but cuz there are two of them and one of you, it sticks.

Learn to think not just mimic what you hear. You're a mental runt calling me a bigot/hater.

BACKSTABBING SLANDERERS

After accusing you of most horrific things counter to your character, they ghost you/disappear.

Then they always come back, giving you a chance to apologize for what they did to you.

BY A THREAD

No one wanted Nietzsche's gift to the world till a century later he's a world famous philosopher.

Never talk to jealous backstabbers bringing up the past again. You've paid your dues now win.

Every herd has it's threshhold limits beyond which novelty brings abuse, but this era's obtuse.

Especially with liberal women, novelty gets attacked and what happens to husbands is sad.

As far as the past goes, it doesn't exist or they're all dead. It was just a level--see that instead.

Learn to stand up for yourself or be under the control of inferior people--freedom vs. evil.

The treated you like nothing cuz without holy spirit you were nothing before the Potter's Wheel.

I had to stop trusting people cuz that was a drip-dry place of total and complete loneliness.

I had to give em all up and turn totally to GOD and in one minute that awful depression lifted.

DISHONOR FROM MEN

I was a different person with a different brain, view and bloodstream, unself-aware and insane.

The things I endured like being dishonored by men--men who didn't know any better amen.

They were just out for themselves and you got in the way. Anyone would do but you were easy.

Since they must be seen as victim they'll perpetuate that narrative/get all against you son.

Never go to one who's already minimized you to validate the abuse, it's always excused.

No matter his enormity against you, the world sees him as the victim and you as crazy/rude.

Narcissists are tremendous liars, distorters of truth and victim players. When it starts, watch out.

LIFE SKILLS: PUSH EM AWAY

What is the Life Skills every child must learn/have naturally? To push people AWAY.

Freezing up when someone crosses a boundary is very common today but gotta learn it, ok?

Life is holographic: it unfolds because of patterns and programs learned before, often tragic.

Without a grounded sense of self you don't know when a boundary's been crossed.

To stick up for yourself you must see what will happen if you don't. It'll get worse, you're toast.

He's mad at me now, I'm without the skill set to push back, I'm in panic mode so I LET IT GO.

You must be taught foresight about what will happen if you don't set this boundary: tragedy.

They're split/black and white thinkers so you're either good or bad, not good AND bad.

He pedestalizes you [you're good] but with one slipup you're now bad and he rages like a wolf.

Now seen as "bad" all his unresolved conflicts land on you who has mercilessly victimized HIM.

BY A THREAD

NARCISSISTIC DEVALUING

Narcissistic devaluing: On Monday I had tremendous value to him but on Tuesday I was nothing.

These guys will always bring up your sin of yesteryears so it's best to relocate and save your tears.

You let him down--he thought your were great but now you've really triggered this clown.

They ignore your adult achievements and talk of your sins of youth: this is the type I knew.

She wasn't a dirty nymphomaniac, she just had no boundaries and that's all it took.

Why did she have no boundaries, allowing easy access? TRAUMA broke the hedge.

Phoning allows people to get onto their narcissistic tangents when you're all business.

They wanna hook you on the horn with them, and it's so boring. I insist on EMAIL ONLY.

They disqualify themselves by bringing up past sins and ignoring achievements, hell with em.

Don't give time/energy to these people who can't get over your past. It's them vs. BLAST.

I'm resilient, I always pop right back up no matter how you obstruct so bud just give it up.

The narcissist always pedestalizes and you always fall off then he's fit to be tied, pissed off.

IT'S PRINCIPALITIES AND POWERS

BY A THREAD

Not people but the consequences of sin and principalities/powers were cruel to you.

Sin is out of order--crooked--and people react. Once in order [repentant] they don't: fact.

There are consequences to sin like their social devices to bring your ruin: Fallen Hero Syndrome.

When finally done with hometown blues and sequestered in the new success comes too.

Once you overcome old system of homeostasis [put-down devices] of the jealous you're adult sis.

Cells give em too much chance to go on and on about themselves, email's most convenient.

Narcissists are phony: their private and public selves don't match but only the wife knows that.

Real recognizes real and fakes flop together. Always recall that when lonely or whatever.

Entire American cities given over to meth and fentanyl--it is shocking how vulnerable we are.

ANGER

Anger mischaracterizes who you are--you're pegged for life due to one minute of bad behavior.

The gentlest most docile may become raging bulls for a split second and are pegged for it.

Think of it: 99% of the time they're gentle/1% mad as hell but that's how they're seen by all.

Sad Failure: They never got to show who they are cuz anger misrepresented their character.

BY A THREAD

Anger will ruin many potentially great relationships cuz it misrepresented your character quick.

One angry man can drive a whole group into hatred and violence. Have no such friendship.

Suppressed anger can turn you into a victimizer--doing mean things not realized till years later.

ANGER SEEDS REPRODUCE

Bury a seed of anger in heart and it reproduces from the start/doesn't help covering it up.

The heart is productive soil--whatever you plant there will reproduce and your dreams are gone.

When an angry victimizer a get-even spirit takes over and now someone's gotta pay, it's war.

Never processed what happened thirty years ago with dad so now you abuse wife instead.

I've only helped you but your unresolved anger made you a victimizer of me and others.

MAL-ADAPTIVE COPING DEVICES

I maladapted to their misjudgment by devices to cope with frustration and got even worse then.

"As an old lady they don't come around to bug me yet before they used me mercilessly."

At every age of my life, suffering, monstrous suffering, was my lot. Nietzsche and Madness

Your lesson by the cad or the shrew: the extent to which a person will go to break you.

There are two ways to understand everything about people: their systems and their levels.

People can't act nor think beyond their level--eventually you see they're just low devils.

People act according to the role in a system. They're enmeshed, that's how you understand em.

A Jezebel stuck in low. self-esteem will act according to how things seem when so jealous see.

JBZEBEL HELL

The Jezebel in your life could never understand you Ace. It's asking a legless man to run a race.

She coulda been killed by the people she had around her but she was still naive, a curse.

I got my Ph.D. in the Streets after leaving my father's house to be victimized by a lush/louse.

Since she could never understand me I had to train her how to treat me which made her angry.

The narcissist is a master at getting all against you and if not strong enough it's your Waterloo.

Suddenly you must defend yourself against misjudgment. You need training until then.

You won't have the necessary boldness until repentance. Until then, utter weakness.

UTTER WEAKNESS

Utter weakness is going along with the current narrative like a parrot, a nut like relatives.

BY A THREAD

When I laid a boundary she'd complain to her flying monkey and I'd be in trouble see.

I held in my frustration at misjudgment for three decades and now it's pouring out like rain.

I literally had to write out an entire theory in psychology to prove her wrong and me right I think.

Face they're the walking dead/pray God wakes em up instead so they'll listen to you the head.

Trust a preacher who's been thru evil and overcame it to choose the right, he's a bright light.

RESISTANCE BUILDS MUSCLE

Thru insult and criticism she provided the necessary resistance to build muscle of a genius.

My Scottish pride prevented me from ever giving up in establishing identity despite enemies.

After a life of adversity and overcoming I'm ready to present. Well almost, still a little diffident.

To find the True Self I entered the deep collective unconscious feeling terrors on all sides.

Not until establishing boundaries to be ALONE was I happy/the most creative star ever shone.

But when I have to adapt to them I lose it totally and become a sad empty shell suddenly.

That's why I say: All you need is a SPOUSE and a LOCKED GATE and your destiny rolls out.

SPOUSE GIVES INDEPENDENCE

BY A THREAD

You need a spouse to be independent otherwise you're chumming with others not worthy of it.

If I'm scared to death of your associates you can bet I'll be disassociating from you/good riddance.

You wanna be a monk? Face yourself by going deep inside and letting the outer go for awhile.

I've been high and popular, I've been low, falling and hated by all. It's cycles and human nature.

Without a spouse you settle for less just to fill your time and it's all so disappointing.

I've been high and popular, I've been low, falling and hated by all. It's human nature/cycles.

He was so depressed after giving the world what it didn't want Nietzsche entered the dark.

It does get depressing being undervalued, dismissed, ignored or misrepresented I declare.

LIBERAL LOSERS ARE USERS

I declare: liberal losers are users and are the most punishing people to be around ever.

Don't let em in cuz they could even kill you to get what they wanted but I lived to tell about it.

What are they doing in your house anyway? They should be away, in their own home ok.

The blame game is a demonic strategy all narcissists use and it can affect your entire identity.

It's where the narcissist makes you responsible for the mess they created and you buy it.

BY A THREAD

They create the problem then reverse the situation so you're to blame for everything, amen.

He cheats on her, she confronts him and he immediately accuses her of doing the same.

He does you dirt but has a peculiar art of twisting that thing around to accuse you first.

JOLLY JIMMY IS A FAKE

Jolly Jimmy was so good at it as a social manipulator I had to scratch my head, am I the loser?

It's demonic: One of the main characteristics of the demonic is accusation then ruin.

Hard times make strong men who make good times which make soft men then hard times.

Helluva situation that the spirit of accusation is the center of the demonic, so learn from it.

While the narcissist hides he puts the victim's supposed faults under giant spotlight.

SYSTEMS AND LEVELS

The way you forgive em is to see it as a system where all parts interlocked in causation.

A person cannot behave beyond their level so see those levels and understand the devil.

Understand their low level and their behavior won't surprise you anymore my jewel.

When you know the nature of a beast its behavior no longer surprises you. Miles Monroe

You have a RIGHT to be happy and move on and the only way is to forgive, so do it now.

Just skip dinner for it's dangerous to choke in your sleep, common asphyxiation extreme.

LOSING HIS HEDGE

As long as hedge is down there's an evil army all around but I believed His promises and won.

When I lost His hedge it was several decades of nuisance/torture from all sides I recollect.

Now He put me behind a locked gate and I can freely do my own thing every day, ALL day.

Seasons are natural--unforced & changing--so wait for your time just around the corner maybe. END END

FEELINGS AND BOUNDARIES

One can't have self-confidence without finding the self first--by laying boundaries, of course.

Sticking up for yourself means you know how you feel and that's what your boundaries reveal.

To survive as a child you may have dissociated from feelings and you continued suppressing.

If your feelings have been suppressed thru alcohol you can't stand up for yourself gal.

By eating your feelings/stuffing em down you're mal-adapting, not standing your ground.

When I laid a boundary he said "but I don't understand" and I FINALLY said "I don't give a dam."

BY A THREAD

It doesn't matter if he understands or not because he was brought up in a barn of nuts.

FEELINGS OF BEING IMPOSED ON

These feelings [of being bothered and imposed upon] are INTENSE--feeling them is your fence.

Yes trauma collapses morals and boundaries but we must work against these tendencies.

It's not a survival mechanism to lay down/let the whole world in but that's what happens.

I was intensely bothered but denied the torture by adapting thru drugs, food, alcohol, whatever.

Without being self-aware you're miserable without knowing why. It's disrespect vs. high.

Disrespect from others is felt deeply and in some like this one proud Scotchwoman, infinitely.

If this stays unrecognized, the addictions covering it over/holding her together are maximized.

You can never please everyone all the time sis so you gotta please yourself like the genius.

When pleased with your own selections its world acclaim, it's people-pleasing before then.

Even if everyone disagrees with you if you push through all will [LATER ON] agree too.

In a world of dummies the genius is called "dumb"-- it's hard to overcome/thrown crumbs.

REGAINING LOST FEELINGS

BY A THREAD

Regaining lost feelings and then setting boundaries on em is called the "Adult Process" friend.

When I got the strength to stand up for privacy needs and throw them out, I became an ADULT.

When I relocated/left all behind I became more adult and my final maturity was getting a wall.

People are out to get you and until you realize that you stay a child without defense/neurotic too.

A child lets everyone in, kids are always with friends and they bring an army to your home.

They let everyone in and are instant friends. I could never understand this insane trend.

BOUNDARY-BUSTERS

A common situation: When someone crosses your boundaries you freeze/don't respond.

A child has no defenses against boundary-busters and I didn't either as a dysfunctional daughter.

They weren't modeled how to have safe conversations with boundaries as a child, that's why.

Parents didn't negotiate fairly with the child so he doesn't even know enough to cry.

If boundaries were shot to hell by sisters and brothers how can she stand against molesters?

"No, I don't like how that feels", "NO, I don't wanna do that"—a child is an adult if he stands up.

As long as she's addicted to crutches she can never lay boundaries and stave off touches.

BY A THREAD

Boundary-assertion is the greatest lesson for youth as it brings self-honor to avoid the uncouth.

RESPONSES TO "NO"

We may have said "NO" but we were gaslit, criticized, mocked, told we've no rights to say NO.

We're missing that chip that automatically says: No, we need to stop and do something else.

The adult says: we need to talk. My boundaries: this is what I'm willing to do, this I'm not.

If you pull Junior High crap on me again & bring all your friends to hell with ya & good riddance.

I will not give in to the traditions of men. It's the stumbling block of the church said Him.

I don't care what they think. All discoveries are artistic, landmark studies show it thru history.

Even discoveries in math and physics are artistic, triggering a paradigmatic gestalt switch.

Discoverers present the matrix then the mere technicians follow by proving segments.

I'm too busy for you, don't come back. You waste all my time then gossip about me: fact.

THEIR RESPONSE IS YOUR RESPONSIBILITY?

A traumatized child feels another's response is their responsibility, e.g. if they're aggressive/angry.

They're accusatory, opinion-forcing, evil gossiping but your job is to smile and be pleasing?

BY A THREAD

As a child my personality trait was "agreeable", starting a life enduring the unacceptable.

As highly agreeable I was highly forgiving until all I thought about was drinking/binging.

I felt it was my job to make em feel better when I fell outa favor & what they're doin', no matter.

If he's accusatory, I should feel responsible and guilty for what's coming out of his mouth.

Someone struggling with a trauma background feels shame, and this person is ANGRY...

I just don't like you and I don't know what it is. It's something inside you and I resist.

TURN THE ATTACK BACK

She insulted and obstructed me so much she drove me to discipline and final world success.

You don't have to be a crazy right-winger to wanna be with your own/not have others around.

I sidestepped the evolutionary march of culture by being 31 years in a wilderness desert.

I didn't age cuz I wasn't exposed to the dirty lifestyle in which the schools had them engaged.

You may win this round but don't forget I always pop right back up again cuz I've got HIM.

I was caught in his trap of control and counter-control while everything was coercive/fearful.

After being with a. controlling narcissist freedom is all I wanna have and all I wanna be, amen.

BY A THREAD

Freedom not to feel shame--his game. Freedom to think/say what I want, not called lame.

JEALOUS NARCISSISTS

It's a black nightmare to be with a controller when you're meant to be free, believe me.

I can still recall the pit in my gut from the evil environment, it was imprisonment.

I was caught in a vice always thinking what will he do to me next? Remember, he was JEALOUS.

I got away from a man with a female-hating streak in him, and one with a stable of women.

For I compete with no one: NO ONE. I'm number one or you are only invisible to me, in sum.

All it took was a relationship with a jealous narcissist to teach me more than a library of books.

FREEDOM IS MARRIAGE BEHIND A WALL

FREEDOM is marriage in a home behind a wall or locked gate. Everything else is slavery.

Being single sucked--they all wanted a piece of me and were angry, aggressive, controlling.

The women were the worst controllers, coming in not to befriend but to ruin me/push me over.

I'm not against all men, I feel sorry for them. Both sexes are now controllers, it's the trend.

I feel for men cuz women ruin them in divorce and 70% initiate proceedings: a home-killing.

What about the kids and pets? They lose their home too, all cuz women divorce to follow suit.

One friend divorces then they all do it. Seeing it as an achievement--when everyone loses?

All narcissists play the victim role. That means you're constantly accused/made into a mule.

Someone to protect you so you do your own thing unviolated by the outer/corny/intrusive world.

It's scary that men are putty in the hands of clever jezebels even thinking like those people.

Yes it's telepathic and that's the way I want it. Words are inadequate just avoid the lunatics.

They're the hero, you're the defective one--that's the story the narcissist tells everyone.

They always set the stage that they're the victim of you, so with trouble you're in full view.

IF YOU DARE COMPLAIN

If you dare complain you're a drama queen or an ingrate, that's your daily conditioning.

After constantly being shut down like your feelings don't matter you can't process them either.

You deny them/suppress them but you still **FEEL** them and there's an ocean below growing.

Pretending you're not angry makes things worse as you become more depressed/anxious.

Try to please the gossiper behind the veil and you invalidate yourself/will certainly fail.

BY A THREAD

He was laying evil seeds against me to everyone yet I was shutting my mouth, agreeable again.

DON'T BE DIFFICULT

I'd been programmed to fear being seen as "difficult"-- so exhausted, agreed to be seen as a nut.

Brainwashed from childhood to fear opening my mouth I finally exploded to tell the world all.

Always happy when alone, when involved I was put through a ringer and swallowed up.

I was conditioned to fear being called "difficult" and that was a big lock on my mouth.

"Difficult" was the buzz word and I was seen that way by everyone in the cult and what an insult.

The sisters stayed agreeable to not lose validation but they were the unlucky ones, dumbed.

These social devices are the workings of a family system, like an interlocking corporation.

Interlocking jealousy patterns: there's no stamping out these fires but walking away surely inspires.

UNPROTECTED SINGLENESS

Any woman choosing to be single is taking her life in her own hands and it's dangerous man.

Choose well, that's for sure, minding these principles of systems theory that kill your allure.

You mocked my theories and ridiculed me to your group so no, no interviews with you.

BY A THREAD

For I have been thru hell with people: they are the problem in a system or chain of evil.

The mindless attacks stopped the day I got married so yes, it's essential to fulfill your destiny.

A controversial/inconvenient woman is attacked if single but if married put on a pedestal.

People are cruel but you don't feel it if rich, popular, etc. I've been on the lower in America.

People are narcissists--if you've got something they want or elevates them then they're nice.

But the minute you fall it's the Fallen Hero Syndrome where your best fans try to kill you man.

In order to write books on What People Are Like I had to endure excruciating social pain, yikes.

The narcissist lays the groundwork with everyone who knows you then suddenly you're screwed.

THEY ALWAYS TELL EVERYONE

He gets the landlady on his side, she calls the sheriff to confide then they all show up one night.

The Opinion Leader of the tribe doesn't like you--you're a thinker who is out of control.

She's a genius at setting fires all around you, she's busy on the horn all day and night too.

Being caught in a system with that witch was like being in a vice and I became nervous/got an itch.

All I can say is God saved the queen and gave me an escape route--every time I got out.

BY A THREAD

My life was cursed being around those people but it wrote many books on psychology of evil.

Even my own mother was always aggressin' but at least she bought me trumpet lessons.

The pain is deep but it keeps me clear & grateful I never have to go thru that again, fateful.

NARCISSISTS AND CALUMNY

Narcissist sets the stage of how they're a victim of you so you can't complain to others too.

The narcissist feminist has already set the stage with all that they're the victim of YOU.

Will-reading time reveals sister already made the lawyer know she's your victim--let it go.

Your tendency to get back fast: I promise you if you wait on the Lord it's the GREATEST vengeance.

False religion is everywhere and I'm talking about Mr. and Mrs. Social Charm: church elders.

My job was to bring a sword just like Jesus and this has made life very rocky tho' I profited.

PRINCIPALITIES AND POWERS

It helps to now it's not them you're fighting but the principalities & powers behind them.

See the power behind em not the person or you'll naturally take vengeance-- no good son.

As long as you're weak the evil powers will trip you up and it's always people who obstruct.

BY A THREAD

Repent of your sins and you're no longer enslaved thru shame to frenemies blocking your gains.

Repent and you're clean again, alert and de-confused from the terror by night that ensued.

See through the flashy archetype he played and you'll see a regular guy with NO power ok?

Making Gold is transmuting negative forces into good by purely refusing to give in like you did.

You're not mad at Cindy it's the devil behind her but that's why violence has erupted all over.

Much rejection comes from narcissistic injury that you made it out and they stayed a loser see.

Take the regular guy in the corner, dress him up. Not the archetype of a player who can't stop.

After abuse by dumbed women in a small town my brain took it ALL in--I wrote it all down.

They don't believe what you say. Disbelief is disrespect which you deeply sense ok?

LOSING POWER OF AN ARCHETYPE

Now that he's lost the power of the archetype he was playing out he's just another chump.

Its a sad sight when a narcissist is depedestalized or loses the power of his grandiose archetype.

Instead of asking em if they have a problem know they DO have one: the devil in em hates you.

The narcissist has already spoken to your mother, brother, best friend, employer or whoever.

BY A THREAD

The narcissist seeks control and he always does it through people, that's what I know.

You now see it as inferior cuz "they" didn't like it. It's social hypnotism, reality its the opposite.

The radical left is the most racist group in America and we need to repeat that to all of ya.

"No human being is illegal" says the left which the dumbed down public accepts as real.

Once freedoms are lost they're near impossible to regain so tell the world what I'm sayin'

Do not rely on people. it's great when encouraging but what happens when they flake out?

ALL THAT torment I went thru with people wrote 130 books on social psychology so I'm grateful for it all, truly.

Adversity builds INSTINCTS and whether social muscle or brain power, hard circumstances creates genius.

Stronger, more capable of handling extreme upsets, surviving what comes at them--these are the champions.

NAME DROPPERS ARE BORING

The king on the mountain doesn't worry over rejection or disapproval by those on the bottom.

My vindictive haters took the music player off and sabotaged the sequences, help God!

You block me baby and i'll block you back so if you change your mind its too bad sad sack.

You brought too dam many people around here and that's what I couldn't stand about you sir.

BY A THREAD

How completely presumptuous to bring your people to my house. The flying monkeys of a louse.

I'll decide who comes into my home not you, this is my spiritual sanctuary you buffoon.

You're always name-dropping and it's so boring let alone something I'd be adoring darling.

Hey, you would never do this on your own, you're just trying to get approval from the woke.

So I'm supposed to respect you cuz you know all those people? We're in different worlds evil.

I'VE MATURED, YOU MAKE ME SICK

I've finally matured, you make me sick. I see it all differently and it happened quick.

I'm like Blanche in Streetcar Named Desire. Hypersensitive and abused by gross liars.

At times I was like Martha in Who's Afraid of Virginia Wolf but we'll forget all that said God.

I'm not into long circuitous paragraphs but sentences and sequences whether music or words.

I pushed thru the birth of the Creative Act thru a seven day fast and everything's different at last.

If you show mercy to others after all they did to you then God will show mercy to you too.

Sometimes I feel artists are too busy describing their work rather than just doing it, a kinda cover up.

He was a merchant of misery coming with his army, stealing from me, making me unfree.

BY A THREAD

ADAPTANTS IN YOUR HOME

Whenever someone's in your home you gotta adapt to their personality and honey, no way.

Cats and dogs love the music so give em a break and turn off the cacophonous TV so chaotic.

MAN and MEN are nonpersonal pronouns referring to ALL mankind so stop your silly whine.

It came from an Early Trauma and you don't have to know what it was. Just know it/look up.

SUPERIOR does not refer to skin or race but how you act and think--and is it efficacious?

The left's offended with Manual for SUPERIOR MAN but that's how I forced the contradiction.

I could write a library of books on mental illness cuz I went through it and didn't even know it.

I could write a library of books on compulsions, obsessions, antipathies and possessions.

These mental illnesses as I had come from TRAUMA and it's a fine science now, the fall outs.

Due to the TRAUMA the mental illness was my blind spot and I couldn't see what others saw.

It was a shocking thing for sure and it isolated me more and more but opened me up to explore.

TRAUMA = FATAL MENTAL ILLNESS

This fatal mental illness involved me with bad characters and I didn't even know any better.

BY A THREAD

As I used crutches to cope with my anxieties a different personality took over--the false self.

As the years went on my illness became more obdurate until I had to break out or whither and die.

Early trauma becomes a blind robot just to hold inner splits together, e.g. relying on liquor.

Thru' an inner journey for years and solitude I became self- and God-aware as they go together.

I felt terrified around the other kids, sick. Liquor, food and sex seemed to be everyone's fix.

I felt homesick, terrified, appalled and lonely in a crowd. I now see it was liberalism's flaws.

All that sex is sick and you can't see it, it's supposed to be only a private thing in marriage.

I had a mental illness but was able to do this work in spite of it to compensate/cover for it.

Despite being raped by Dad 200x by age ten she became the biggest evangelist friend.

NO NURTURANCE FROM OLD REJECTORS

Don't seek nurturance from past rejectors who have disqualified themselves [not your friends].

Stop seeking nurturance from old rejectors, stop trying. Shut that door, you'll be high.

Have the class not to write an old rejector. Just thinking about that is a real bummer.

Early trauma brings anosognosia where part of your brain is blocked off until you wake up.

BY A THREAD

We all have talents and slice of the pie, there is no competition. It's your own stream man.

I don't know why God chose me as a vessel for this Creative Act but we're all one in fact.

I know all about being so crazy you do strange things and can't help it or even realize it.

You've lost control of the vessel, you're now a possessed robot impressed by people.

Whenever you think of writing someone always ask yourself is he/she an old rejector?

Her Germanic mom was cruel, spiteful and mocking, laughing in her face while torturing.

Turn your back on the past entirely--shut that old door. Look forward to eternity and more.

HE HAS THE TABLE ALREADY PREPARED

The nation is falling, the borders collapsing. It's all due to sin and no repenting: sex, murder, false religions.

As things go sour people get into sin more. It's palliative, a coping device--but gets worse 'til a whore.

As things go sour that's when to repent! God's word says He's changed His mind before, like Nineveh.

Doesn't matter what they think, God has it all lined up. Keep honoring Him, being your best, doing right.

So that He can meet your needs and give you the desires of your heart, so that you may enjoy your life.

The breakthrough is already all set up for you.

BY A THREAD

The people most critical of me were into sex sins or infidelity. That was all ok to the phony peanut gallery.

My biggest hater left his wife with four kids for a mistress. But that was all-ok even with the churches.

Read God's word to see history is CYCLICAL--all depending on what we do. Sin = destroyed soon.

BULIMIA IS A FATAL MENTAL ILLNESS

Bulimia is a mental illness tho' they put em down for this. It's an ugly thing but there's so much more to it.

Bulimia is labeled the most fatal of all mental illnesses so we must look beyond the surface.

Bulimia as a mental illness stems from childhood when self-hate began with an unworthy image.

It's a crippling mental illness but is seen as a vanity thing when it's so much deeper/often unconscious.

Bulimia is a silent empire across the world just as is pornography. A hidden sin tho' pandemic.

Bulimia is such an ugly thing on conscience, guilt and shame needles em for life long after repentance.

Bulimia is a mental illness characterized by irrational guilt and shame after repentance with most.

An ex-bulimic filled with shame and guilt is relieved to know it is a mental illness beyond them.

Bulimia is labeled now as the MOST lethal mental illness with 18 times more suicide and death.

LOW SELF-WORTH STARTS IN INFANCY

BY A THREAD

It starts with some shakeup in infancy giving a self-image of unworthiness, inferiority and negligence.

It's a downward spiral but also an overcompensation for identity thru over-achievement and perfection.

It is such an ugly/embarrassing illness the lasting shame and guilt is inevitable and with age more so.

It's mental illness not a self-absorbed, vain, narcissistic attention-seeker. it's a sad person possible suicider.

There are genetic predispositions that roll out symptoms or social conditions these books describe.

I was born with much incredible energy but it all got blocked by mommy who was always mad at me.

Where did all that energy go? It was blocked then channeled into all addictions even love.

Why was mommy always mad at me? Well it was due to alcohol to which she had a dangerous allergy.

ALCOHOLIC ANOREXIA

Anorexia is often combined with alcoholism. AA: Alcoholic Anorexia. Extremely dangerous.

They may call it "beer fasting": just drinking beer for two weeks and stunts like that with common death.

Would someone who hadn't suffered a broken attachment trauma bond be acting like that? Certainly not.

The sensual/psychoactive/fasting anorexics are on a proprioceptive journey feeling like magic.

It's an embarrassing mental illness but an illness nevertheless--let that relieve your stress.

BY A THREAD

Old cycles end just as new cycles open up. Expect great changes and fast while you strut your stuff.

HATRED OF SOCIAL OCCASIONS

The sad part about having this mental illness is the hatred it triggers in every single social linkage.

But if everyone hates you you will get stronger than the others in dealing with it, so thank you sis.

Attachment injury can bring chronic depression whether you have cars, a house, money or education.

I don't like social occasions. I find them irritating, boring and wounding--who wants to take a chance?

The women sizing me up, the men taking jealous pot shots. Enjoy Christmas, who needs this?

In tyrannical environments you can't criticize a thing. If you do you're out or you'll get a punishing.

SOCIAL CIRCUITRY VS. RECLUSIVITY

Some are automatically hooked thru social circuitry while those who are not are always panicking.

When shown it's a mental illness, for the first time she was able to talk about her secret: bulimia.

When able to discuss this secret all the tension dropped from her being and she was "enlightened".

Lady said "I didn't realize I was mentally ill, I just thought I was a jerk" and she had lived with that.

Once the festering secret hits the light of day all that darkness goes away. It's an ILLNESS ok?

BY A THREAD

Bulimia is **DEFINED** by shame and guilt. It comes before and after until the end of life if without help.

Something happened to make her feel unworthy, like she didn't measure up or wasn't good enough.

It seemed like everyone got along garrulously instantly and I was the misfit odd girl out naturally.

It seemed like everyone knew everyone else's name. I was so impressed with that, I knew none.

I felt inferior all my life cuz I didn't fit but now I see they're twits and I'm really way above it.

It's not the social world which is superior but the spiritual and natural one triggering creativity in us all.

The social world wastes time. Despite connections when you die you'll never see em again.

The bulimic inherits the "critical self" always imposing the damaged image-- substitute with understanding.

THOUGHT-SUBSTITUTION

I know no one's name cuz I don't live in that reality. There's another one inside more fascinating.

It was self-compassion and thought substitution that helped me the most in my health restoration.

It used to be Satan's on my shoulder the minute I awoke but now I block the thought and re-route it.

Take mind out of embarrassment/humiliation into a brand new higher station away from the herd man.

You will **NOT** hold me down with memory anymore for you are my adversary who I'm done with forever.

BY A THREAD

After all I went through--after I'm all new--you will **NOT** hold me down with memories of it too.

Saw an old high school friend and we were light years apart/different planets so I ditched him.

Are people overtaken by mental illnesses or demons? I remember companionship with bedlam.

What is a "lethal mental illness"? One where you are killing yourself but cannot see it.

ANOSOGNOSIA IS LETHAL

My secondary illness was **ANOSOGNOSIA**: being insane and killing myself without being able to see it.

Hell if I'm gonna go thru all that, all those horrid lessons I had to learn about man, and recall it all too.

The devil's not gonna torture me twice: first by being your victim, twice by memories of such vermin.

Mental illness is from other people: by dirty rats attracted in but first when not loved when little.

You advertised for "light housekeeping" but meant "live-in whore". Men like you are the lowest of the low.

Those memories are engraved deep within me to stay away from the enemy and his treacheries.

Stop talking about sex my friend. Who wants to conger you with whomever thrashing around in bed.

MENTAL ILLNESS BY OTHER PEOPLE

Since mental illness is caused by other people recovery is a process of de-peopling and it's a good thing.

BY A THREAD

I was a cute kid but what I witnessed in one moment was so horrible/appalling/shocking I started dying.

Even though you're younger than me I feel like I'm with an old man and I don't wanna go back into that.

The devil uses "professionals" like you. Hippies who became counselors/blind leading blind too.

First you have mental illness from guilt/shame implants then anosognosia: blindness to it.

If I weren't married I'd be so scared. What single decent women have to go through is just plain weird.

Sex: You mean he should test her like a car? Or if she's no good later he's a right to return to Barb?

They use their platform to get women but personally got little goin' for them: dull Elmer Fudds, lemons.

MARRIAGE IS A BEAUTIFUL WALL

Marriage is a wall to keep creepy people out. It works like magic in a second so let out a shout!

God watched as all decency, protocol and diplomacy were suddenly lost and these were my in-laws?

You have prisons then you have the control of other people which is also suffocating and evil.

The saint said "I got so sensitive I couldn't be around priest or profane, it was all too much for me."

Why the hell would I wanna go to your page you boring fool? I'll not waste my time anymore, whew.

You never deserved that self-condemnation you heaped on yourself daily so now start self-soothing.

BY A THREAD

I cried to God about my guilt/shame not knowing from where it came and He said replace the same.

You only need ONE to love and confirm you, not giving a dam what the others think. That's perfect.

Moving the hell outa liberal California was my greatest accomplishment in life: new system/no strife.

After being a weasel all it took was love and I blossomed--the little rejected girl inside they'd been mockin'

I'm learning to replace thoughts that come with PTSD in the night or when I wake up, intrusively.

EMBARRASSMENT/SHAME ACCEPTANCE

Embarrassment, shame and humiliation must be accepted before you can proceed, unfortunately.

Let this be the Day of Humiliation then just go ahead. When we die there'll be no memory friend.

Never forget the greatest geniuses and saviors in their fields began as asses, that's the archetype.

The utter shame and humiliation of doing such a ridiculous thing is usually overwhelming.

Relax, it was a mere thorn in your side. What began as a mountain became a tiny molehill deep inside.

It was a mental illness--you couldn't help it. It became social and fatal because it was genetic.

Better stay low cuz they will hurt you. It's a different age and if you say something they don't like, pow.

Now say it: It was genetic and I couldn't help it and I'm very sorry to anyone connected to it

BY A THREAD

The shame and humiliation of it--this demon who had me in his grip spiraling down in a life so tragic.

And now all that is in the mere back forty? I feel so fortunate for that, God's sin-erasing.

You destroyed my privacy over and over again with all your friends but I've learned my lesson.

HANGING ON TO PAST PEOPLE

You've recovered from trauma but hang on to someone you've always known as a touching stone--NO.

Hanging on to someone you've known is like home but it's a mirage hon'-- they're different/usually liberal.

Returning to your old place won't work either--everything changes/it was magnetism not that situation.

If you can't understand anything it's not my fault. I don't have to explain it over and again you nut.

So they can't see what you see/don't have your tastes, so you're alone--don't suicide over it, buck up.

Hanging on to someone you've known is gonna disappoint big time and soon-- avoid this silly notion.

Obama was glib, that's all. Through masterful chicanery he tried to destroy the country and sell us out.

Many have PTSD/intrusive memories but don't realize it. They drink/distract to cover it but suffer over it.

NO PAST EQUALS WORLD RENOWNED

The beauty of starting all over again and forgetting the past no matter what: this is world renowned.

65

BY A THREAD

Your work is too imperfect. There's too much mixture and a lot of incidental stuff should be rejected.

I don't give a dam about this or that. This leaves me unsatisfied--get a life, get down to facts.

I had a liberal art teacher who walked around with her nose in the air shouting edicts/being a scare.

Seeing it as social/genetic allows acceptance so you go on ahead. As for the others, they're dead.

Yes it was hell--them dropping in--but there are worse things. Study holocaust, get perspective hon'.

Be thankful for everything you have but also realize how fast you can lose it all. Love and be careful.

Human networks can be so obdurate and cruel sometimes you must relocate to co-create as God rules.

It's an accomplishment to strategically relocate. Study it out, get it all together, move and re-adjust.

THE WORLD HATES THE DEVIL IN YOU

Jezebel was so dangerous I had to cut her out completely. I never knew what she'd do so destructively.

The devil's in you cuz you had no boundaries. That was it, no problem, just lessons from the old days.

The world came against the devil in you, not so much you, but it's a very hard thing to deal with too.

Don't let em in and especially don't let em around your children or pets. Trust no man the bible says.

Now start self-soothing. Think of what you've been thru while in denial, love yourself, start creating.

BY A THREAD

Stop the. virtue signaling without knowing anything, it's such a turnoff--also the false ingratiating, yuk!

A narcissist isn't someone who loves himself. He's empty wavering with whoever he wants to impress.

A narcissist mom seems meek but will yank her daughter from her lessons that would make her great.

I'm always happy when I'm working, doing my thing. I noticed that as a teen/was never the same.

The same creepy sisters wrecking your rep will now bloat with pride in reflected glory being your friend.

STOP SAYING "UNITY" IS THE WAY

According to systems theory a true emotional cut-off should dissolve symptoms but it takes time.

This work is not a "downer" but a description of human nature keeping each other down forever.

If you don't wanna blame siblings chalk it up to birth order--whatever it was interrupting your future.

RECOGNIZE SINS OF DETRACTORS

Recognize sins of your detractors. Are they culturally approved sins--are they getting away with murder?

They made me feel so ashamed for being different. But these very people left their dear wives for a slut!

Every time I let someone stay on the ranch i regretted it. Not just them, but their stuff, friends and relatives.

People abuse you with their stuff and people. They impose it all on you but only the strong assert against evil.

BY A THREAD

They're always so nice when they ask to stay. Then they bring a truckload of trouble after you say "ok".

I let one lady in who said she wanted solitude. Once in, all the men in the town came to see the silly nude.

I allowed a man to stay who said he loved nature.   He dragged in unsightly crap and created disorder.

ALL LIFE IMPOSED ON BY PEOPLE

All my life I was imposed on by people. Now that I'm finally free I will never rent so please don't ask me to.

This isn't the fifties when people loved decency. But these guys know nothing about respect for privacy.

They thank you for giving em a space in nature but then keep knocking on your door for cell-phone charger.

They will **NOT** leave you alone tho' they say they love nature. They don't see nature they just wanna chatter.

It's the same with false church: YAK, YAK, YAK! You should shut-up in the sanctuary but they just can't.

The false churchist says you don't love God if you don't wanna socialize with the church: dogma FLAWED.

I spent decades in the desert for my ideas. But even way out there they'd always seek me out, pissed.

You can't stop people from burning wood in a country neighborhood but it's often trash, plastics too.

That's why I'm sick as a dog every day from 4 pm-midnight when I'm ok cuz the burnings have died.

Government tells people to build/rent lodgings in their backyard--it's communism and it's next door.

BY A THREAD

How easily people chum-up without vetting. This isn't the fifties kiddies--you can't trust anyone sweeties.

They wanna make you feel guilty for not renting but they're just communist pawns of Agenda 21, nasty.

Guilty for not renting--like you should be ashamed for your privacy! Privacy is a constitutional right, mighty.

SHAME FOR LETTING EM IN

Ashamed for not letting people into your home? Are you kidding? Everyone's on probation if you're vetting.

Someone came to my home and once in, ten more people appeared! Unbelievable, worse than weird.

Instead of seeing how disrespectful of privacy they are, they call you a hater cuz you don't want em here.

I am not a misanthrope--I don't hate people but what the left has made em. We are to be excellent.

I make believe DALLAS is my family or Bonanza is my brothers protecting me: The therapy of fantasy.

Just like Sodom and Gomorrah it's one big orgy. Don't believe the surface these people are dirty.

Middle aged women partaking in wet tee-shirt contests and gross things like that--boob jobs/endless chat.

Privacy is a CONSTITUTIONAL right darnit. That makes it ultra-important to us Americans, so get/stay out.

Now I see why mom was pist when I brought friends home. She hadn't vetted em and she was forlorned.

BEING ALONE IS HIDEOUS TO THEM

She just wanted to be alone and didn't want anyone in her home! It's contact equals conquest/no fun.

God wrote it and had the link too.

When they go into the hospital it's one big social so the wife sleeps there to be socially available.

The superior life is the inner one yet these people have NO inner life--they will suffer if alone tonight.

Communists are always pressuring you to rent, to relax and lose your privacy, to spend more time with em.

I resent the pull to rent or making me feel guilty cuz I don't want that. This is the communist spirit!

Commune-ism. Grouping up, shacking up, chumming up rather than just being alone and enjoying lunch.

When you are at that level of greatness the success and money will come, it is inevitable hon'.

The Millennials personified by AOC are entitled, stupid and weak. Adversity makes ya stronger creeps.

What I went through invaded in a small town made me strong: building muscle to manage throngs.

Tho' intimidated by social setups, status-tension and aggression my adversities made me master of em.

And now I see it had to happen, every bit of it. I was a limp noodle in boundary assertion/a real twit.

Realizing how much adversity empowered me removed my resentments at the actors oppressing me.

ANTI-WHITE RACISM

BY A THREAD

Saying "it's bad to be white" is total racism. What the hell is going on? The self-hatred of leftism.

America has its problems but is still the best answer for ALL problems the world faces. Robert Barnes

It proves the vitality of ideas that people seek to shame us for them as idiots--their efficacy scares em.

You planted a helluva seed and it all happened as if by decree so of course God'll bless your work sweetie.

Waiting in faith builds more muscle than even dealing with those creeps invading me without cease.

I knew they didn't understand me--how could they? They were hix when it came to social psychology.

HAD TO PLAY THEIR GAME

I had to play their game and go along just to not be beaten up. The young left are bristly, angry, violent.

They'll kill your dog to get back at you. These are liberal "animal lovers" but everything turns out cruel.

What I went thru--being thrown in a shark tank--made me super-protective of home, hearth and family/pets.

They are so slovenly, careless, un-thorough, heedless and distracted into pure folly while being angry.

It wasn't Borrego it was that level of weakness acting as a magnet to controllers and other wickedness.

FEMINISTS GANG UP ON THE RECLUSE

As a newbie to a desert town the feminists grouped up and attacked me, some violently and one was 53.

BY A THREAD

They didn't like me unique and happy as a lark in my desert solitude and I found them dumb, rude, crude.

The more I knew em the more disgusted I would become. When cut off by God, there's always somethin'.

Cut-off by God they have no power so must pull you down like crabs in a bucket and I cried "come Lord".

They simply can't leave you alone. They're compelled to torment you until you're more like them, boring.

Use adversaries to compete against in order to pull yourself up--works like a charm, then they're gone.

SHOOOTING AT SHADOWS

Shooting at shadows: Once you're in safe circumstances you can't believe things could be this peaceful.

I still have PTSD from what they did to me but now that I see the MUSCLE it built I accept the tragedy.

I can't compete with anyone at all, I'm in my own separate reality and world-- it's maturity after being ruined.

He calls himself a philosopher and writer when he's really a go-fer--still entangled and also a sinner.

They judged me for not having many friends. But if involved in your destiny, who has time for em?

My husband, my pets, one tech and neighbor once in awhile--the rest is destiny, thrilling inner journey, style.

You're so dam socially hypnotized it makes me sick and I'm not putting up with it: Say that to the twits.

I love this writer's level playing field. I love that all I need is cash conduit to my card/never be interviewed.

BY A THREAD

PROMOTION NOT FROM PEOPLE

Promotion not from people, it comes from the Lord--this releases any need to suckup to the mob.

The less you depend on people, the greater the anointing on your life.

For giant success for your convictions you must stay energetic in your anticipations--don't lose em!

I lost my joy, gave up my hopes and dreams--the result of listening to negative people or the obscene.

No matter how ridiculous your vision, hold onto it. No matter how long it's been taking, anticipate success for it.

All downswings in my life came from CONTACT = CONQUEST. Had I stayed alone I'd stayed my best.

Maybe my words'll be read long after I'm dead--the most important being: it's people you should dread.

When God designed the plan for your life He gave you everything you need to fulfill it. The link? No sweat.

Every good break, every person, solution or coincidence is already set up--He's not trying to figure it out!

He's already set up the promotion. The impossible problem has a solution designed before the problem.

THE IMPOSSIBLE DREAM IS ALREADY HERE

The impossible dream and all solutions are already in your future, waiting for you in the wings.

If you stay in faith--not let negative voices talk you out of it--you'll come in to God's predesigned plan.

The table will already be set up. You won't need to ask, they're ready to fill your cup. It's predesigned, look up!

God is omniscient--He sees the future, we cannot. Trust Him on everything, He said He'd destroy the rot.

When you live in faith expecting God's goodness there will be moments of favor and SUDDEN blessings.

I was a happy healthy creative kid but at 15 they laid this white privilege crap on me and I degraded quickly.

Because of my white tendency to order and express higher concepts they attacked me mercilessly.

The whole thing is just amazing to me. Thesis, antithesis = synthesis, I HAD to go through all of this.

I always felt predestined for something. The only time I didn't was due to sinning = lost destiny/catastrophe.

I was so eclipsed by other members (feminists) that I degraded for decades and lost life, my sense of it.

Forget what you went thru with scoundrels they were just there to educate boundaries around you.

God has right people in right positions for you. You don't have to have favor with all, just the right one!

THEY ARE IRRELEVANT NOW—LET EM GO

They are totally irrelevant now. They will be cut off, destroyed. God said it in Psalms and I am amazed.

Bring back the stories where crime doesn't pay. Show the masses how God works each and every day.

They are "prepared blessings" that you have not seen, heard nor imagined.

Sometimes there's a blessing already set up and people will talk you out of it, reasoning it couldn't happen.

BY A THREAD

My mother couldn't see it, but God didn't put it in her heart. Jus cuz loved ones can't see it, don't depart.

It's a giant release to not care that I sell. I've done my work for the Lord and that alone thrills my soul.

To not have boundaries when people are imposing on you is like a rudderless boat and quicksand too.

Only by repenting of my sins did I gain boundaries to wall the devilish, imposing, thieving world out.

Without repentance it's like God is using your invaders as punishers. See it like that to rid bad memories.

Without repentance God uses invaders as punishers: See it like that to rid remorse, I swear it works.

When you finally see the system between your sins and consequences (karma) you'll see you deserved it.

SEE THE SYSTEM THEN LET IT GO

See you deserved it = able to let it go, finally. Now go into the already setup blessings waiting for you.

God has lined up divine connections: people who will go out of their way to show you favor, amen.

It's all about imposing people on ya: wicked men hypnotizing weak women in their homes, mass immigration.

It was the Baptist lady convincing me I should be good and let these pre-convict boys into my home.

It was the Mormon lady moving me to forgive without requiring justice or just forget how they messed up.

It was the false church lady demanding I attend boring social meetings to show I'm a godly lady.

BY A THREAD

No I don't wanna go to your kissy-huggy prayer group that waits for stragglers and is like a chicken coop.

Your problem is total conformity to some norm but the problem is that norm keeps changing: alarm.

State the truth BOLDLY. It's a world dying for what you have, URGENTLY. Must repent/return to NORMALCY.

Resolution: I'm NOT gonna look at the scales and I'm NOT gonna look at my sales--God has the details.

The people who are your link to success have already been set up, God has prepared their hearts.

PRISON PREPARATION THEN ERASE EM

Prison prepared many disciples but their problem was memories of these lesson-learning obstacles.

I don't wanna keep thinking back to those horrible things I confronted, to learn what God predesignated.

I had to learn what the world was all about--what people were like, what they had become: moral scum.

They were lower than animals due to their behavior from sin. It's a door way to demons without limits.

KIDS ARE DEMONS WITHOUT LIMITS

That's the kids: demons without limits. Cuz who's to say? Take God out and you have wanton debauchery.

Once you remove these demons from your life God spreads a table of goodies when free of this strife.

When God has ordained someone to help you, they don't have to like you.

It doesn't matter if they don't like you cuz God controls the universe and they won't have a choice.

BY A THREAD

If it's already set up, bad breaks can't stop it, nor injustice, nor petty people--you're right on schedule.

The link is gonna find you. You're not gonna have to find it, it's gonna come to you even by accident.

Don't bemoan past mistakes or people cuz it built spiritual muscle and that's about borders against evil.

When it doesn't work out your way it's because God has something better. Move with this, remember.

Closed doors are like God's doing us a favor.

What God has designed for you is far more rewarding and fulfilling than petty plans which are so limiting.

THANK YOU FOR WHAT YOU'VE ALREADY DONE

Instead of bemoaning disappointments say "Father thank you for the blessings You've already set up!"

Lord thank you for the good breaks, healings, promotions and the right people You've already ordained.

Since it's all meme with nothing behind it, they can't debate the issue and will only/always split the scene.

I think complexly and they think appetitively, basically. It's all instinct--they want what you have, only.

If they can't think and their ancestors lacked critical thinking skills too, they can only react by memes/rote.

SUDDENLY A GREAT CONTACT

SUDDENLY you meet the right person/get the contract. That was one of those blessings God already set up.

They didn't get what you wanted--God has something better for you, that's all you should think about it.

Just as God opens doors that no person can shut, He closes doors that no person can open. Look up

Don't try to re-open old wounds. WHY would you want them back, you fools?

They have *nothing* to give you. Since you last saw em you've skyrocketed while they have degraded.

Their influence so wounded you it built muscle to SHOOT THROUGH the whole bloody lifelong obstacle.

YOU WEREN'T SUPPOSED TO GET IT

If bucked off you weren't supposed to get it. If meant to be yours you can rest assured no one else will get it.

People judge you by the outside, they wanna write you off. They don't see what God put in you, magic elf.

How do you handle being written off? That's what God watches when people don't see your greatness.

PEOPLE: They didn't choose you before in the womb, they didn't have great things set up for you.

God loves to champion people that others discount, discredit, say "they made too many mistakes".

What God has already set up for you will cause them to stand in total disbelief.

They never dreamed you could be that blessed, that successful, that healthy, that free. It's their irony, see?

SEE THE ROT OR PART OF IT

They were absolutely horrible, don't tell me they were not--or it means you are part of this rot.

You're all a bunch of devilish sluts and the men are male sluts! Demons going to hell and on earth, debunked.

BY A THREAD

The fake preachers won't tell you that, they'll allow you to go to hell if you're under their deacon spell.

They see you with all your limitations not a vision of God's blessings catapulting you to new levels.

"HOW DO YOU KNOW IT WILL SELL? WHAT ARE YOU GONNA DO? YOU CAN'T DO THAT! THAT DOESN'T MEAN ANYTHING!"

No person seen, heard or imagined what God prepared for those who love Him: promotion you didn't see coming.

NO ONE COULD EVER IMAGINE

A dozen people may not like you but they can't stop you. God has already set it up while they go down too.

How many past abusers are now dead? God punishes wickedness, believe it.

The problem is: God didn't put the dream in them, He put the dream in YOU. Take no advice/ignore it too.

They can't see what you see, nor feel what you feel. They're in the ordinary natural while God is planetary!

So blessings find you, don't seek the blessings--seek God as first place so the blessing seeks you.

Seek first the kingdom and all these things [ALREADY PREPARED] will be added unto you. Jesus

Joseph's brothers were jealous of him and threw him in a pit. Left him to die then sold him for pittance.

Before he had the problem, the solution was en route. God said in Isiah: Before you called I will answer you.

That problem you're upset about--God already has the solution en route.

You can't see how it could happen but God wouldn't give you this dream or put the promise in you, see?

BY A THREAD

He wouldn't have put this dream in you without already setting up how to bring it to pass. SO RELAX.

WRITING IS ABOUT COPY NOT ME

Writing is about the COPY so you never have to see me. It's not about me it's just COPY for eternity.

Sparta 300 where the kid is sent out to live with the wolves in order to become a champion and the best.

God needed you to be stronger and to survive in a difficult environment so that the others could live.

So I was thrown into a small desert liberal town with a bunch of pigs and hogs and I overcame it all.

In order to protect a huge mass of people God had to train you in the most difficult of circumstances.

I had to learn how to protect my self, mind, stuff, home, pets and my very reality from liberal hogs and pigs.

When constantly attacked and threatened you get accustomed to it then muscle through it, overcoming it.

What a release to see how adversity built strength rather than being angry, resentful or maudlin about it.

Entitled, stupid and weak: leftists on university campuses. Brains wiped out by fantasies and false dogma.

They don't have the independence of thought and spirit to keep liberty alive so rely on state as their guy.

They aren't smart enough to win at debate so they censure, punish, ruin economically, slur image.

Ostracizing is the major one tactic of the left. Isolate, ban, make the others hate you or see you as less.

BY A THREAD

ALL FAMILIES HAVE AN ODD PERSON OUT

It happens in families where suddenly the odd girl out is gossiped about while they take over her finances.

Finally I'm independent of everybody including whether you like me. It's only God's approval I seek.

Here you moved out to the country for the fresh air but are least likely to get it there. Wood burning

They feel they have a moral duty to confront conservative--whether in public or family they're in the right.

Due to the strength of social hypnotism the "fact" they're in the right leaves no doubt/it's a scary fight.

They're overly dependent on each others advice but it's an echo chamber of the blind leading the blind.

I don't care anything about selling. I did the work for God and that's all that matters, I can rest now.

Jesus said "don't even go to the funeral...for who are your sisters? Only those who loved God".

I'm scared to death of these people and not afraid to say it. You call that racist cuz it's all about narrative.

To adapt to that generation is debasing, conscience-searing, disheartening and totally embarrassing.

The genetic tendency of two-liners has really come through.

SOCIAL PSYCHOLOGY: THE HERD

The social cobweb became so pathologically intricate and treacherous we had to relocate for a new start.

All you can do in these trying times is get to safety. For the wicked man is in denial and is shafted.

81

BY A THREAD

My biggest achievement in life was getting to safety--cutting loose everything behind--then enjoy the ride.

Make yourself apt to receive by getting rid of everyone with something up their sleeve--now, succeed.

It's not that people are terrible but that your weakness is a magnet to their wickedness or weirdness.

The superior man is creative all day putting things where they belong and removing things that don't.

MASCULINE is: Channeled aggression, stoicism, self-control, ambition, honor and fury when necessary.

WHITE GENOCIDE: The anti-Anglo ideology is dressed up as anti-racism, since the sixties it has been.

He who fights the previous war loses.

As the nation and religion is replaced by economic freedom and social ethics, everything disintegrates.

To sin is to hand over control. They got you now, it's your aura that has become old while enemies find gold.

Just the inner shame and self-disgust alone weakens you so foes take control. It's a budget you fool.

The only way to permanent victory is repentance. God fills your cup, you're back on top--resplendent.

SIN CONTAINS IT'S OWN CONSEQUENCES

God doesn't even have to punish us for sin, it contains its own punishment like guilt and embarrassment.

With guilt or shame all self-confidence is lost--the boldness necessary to overcome and be boss.

There's no way you could win crippled with shame and guilt. Only rightness brings certitude to win.

The notion of "white privilege" also cuts our power in half as its intention is to wipe us off the map.

The RELIGION of liberalism firmly set sees its aims as morally justified and its critics as morally bankrupt.

There is nothing as dangerous as a population convinced of its moral certitude. VertigoPolitix

When a society enters that state of mind it is completely incapable of self-regulating behavior.

We must fight this liberal religion like it's the 15th century church, knowing the pain it inflicts on "heretics".

LIBERALISM IS A POWERFUL RELIGION

The state has its own inquisitors combatting heresy by posing as journalists making em hate the twits.

Elites feel totally justified in carrying out these judgments without any check on their power to do so.

Liberal theocratic state is powerful until the moment it is not. There's an accumulation of crap, cascade, rot.

It's the last to know it: When it finally falls it is because it's already been discredited long before.

The feature of the white man's culture is his imagining, ordering and expressing higher concepts and ideas.

The white man is different by seeing things that are fundamentally wrong and desiring to change it.

FLAT NON-DYNAMIC PERSONALITIES

They possess flat, non-dynamic personalities operating reactively but which are completely programmed.

Liberal traits: an absence of self-developed ideas, a lack of intellectual maturity, auto-hatred of dissidents.

Liberal mind is characterized by inability to see what's happening until it is too late : dead weight/old freight.

Academic gatekeepers place made-up follies before listless minds accepting the whole scheme blind.

Real vs. synthetic personality (externalizing canned phrases with idealistic sentiments) is: NAIVETE.

When naivete's done persistently in agitation there's a big black hole inside and that's the liberal, bonafide.

These soulless young monsters of the left are now agents of almost all human activity in the west.

Social theories and delectable insults on messaging boards created the biggest memes of last decades.

Dumb memes have enabled the New Right to weaponize a mobile, tactically superior postmodern language.

We combat it with anti-mainstream culture jamming that evades censorship with subtle nuanced shifts.

Subtlety, nuances, triggering subconscious analogies rather than calling em a bunch of names like thieves.

ELITE COMMUNICATION IS SUBTLE

Our subtle but ELITE communication style will blitzkrieg modern culture before it dissolves like a vapor.

Our style will be the crucial mainstay against the hostile liberal elite or the democratic creep.

BY A THREAD

Left agents: with no internality, divine agency or capacity for critical thought they'll blow away like chaff.

Without foundation, inner journey or capacity for critical thought they've only memes they bought

Upon questioning the best will say "I don't know" but most react by flat out rejection or walking away.

They are part meme, part void space--but still very dangerous when arranged in a mob in every case.

With these things in mind, take the straight path oh cosmic soldier.

It's the Animating Contest of Liberty which brings definition to your appearance, not like an ugly dunce.

Colonization is universal throughout history but is only explained in the context of the last centuries.

Leftist anthropologists pushed the false notion that white colonialists disturbed the UTOPIA of non-whites.

They want to colonize us--white nations, spaces, literature--with a colored or multi-ethnic presence.

THEY CONSTRUCT MYTHICAL WORLDS

They construct a mythical multicultural prior state that de-colonization will return us to: malicious fictions.

If these malicious fictions go unchecked it will result in the extermination of western civilization.

Liberalism is entirely negative--it is not a reformative force but a disintegrating one and morally it's scum.

The human organism is either true to itself or becomes sick and distorted, a prey to other organisms.

By making us speak their untruths--upon pain of ostracism/loss of income--they create emasculated liars.

The white man is bombarded relentlessly with calls for his capitulation at the altar of anti-white liberalism.

The devastation to white normies is compounded by its adherence controlling all psychiatric institutions.

"Psychology" is now a means of industrializing this gaslighting of white society and western populations.

Evil men and seducers shall wax worse and worse deceiving and [don't forget this part] being deceived.

Gay men and lesbians: it's a spirit not a gene.

To the fray: If you wanna be popular and go on a talk show just come outa the closet and say you are gay.

The seasons are the UNFORCED cycles of nature. That means there's nothing you can do but wait/mature.

The Lord preserves all who love him, but all the wicked He will destroy. Psalm 145: 20

THE GREAT WORK IS COMPLETE, BUT GOTTA WAIT

After you complete the Great Work you still gotta wait. Get your wardrobe together, plan, eliminate.

Waiting is part of the process at the end. This is where persistence wins out and patience is your friend.

You know "it" is going to happen since He took you this far. You are just a conduit but seen as a star.

You know what this is. Just cuz they're too dumb to appreciate it, ignore them for its God's final test.

BY A THREAD

They are so messed up in this era this will be a turkey-shoot, a cakewalk. The harvest is ripe, so talk.

You know it's gonna happen and it could be rough. So appreciate this respite and just hang out.

You know it's gonna happen cuz they're desperately dumb and you spent decades resolving it all.

I spent decades in the desert wilderness figuring this out. Like jealousy triangles and betrayal trauma.

God came thru me for years--every minute I was a conduit. Not to boast, I feel blessed for the Creative Act.

You must anticipate it since that demonstrates faith. You know it's coming but God knows the minute.

Instead of anger over old wounds, keep thinking "sin and punishment" cuz that's what it's all about.

Sin warps your looks and aura acting as a magnet to insults all around--it's a process not a person.

PEOPLE-WORSHIP IS PURE IDOLATRY

They object to my title "People are Cruel" cuz since the sixties we worship people not God: not cool.

No one's good even Jesus said that. People can be scoundrels--they all got something the dirty rats.

Idolatry is a major sin: people-worship. That's why all the kissin' and huggin' for show, so you'll know it.

Without the true God they have a big hole inside. So they cling to each other even if the one has lied.

What people think is 0% and what God thinks is 100% so why even bother with em? Rely on the Lamp.

BY A THREAD

From what I read in the Psalms, you gotta be HAPPIER than on the day He rewards you. I get it, so cool!

They escape to the desert only to buy a track home surrounded by multitudes of similitude so boring.

I took an old cabin way, WAY out. I wanted no neighbors at all/those who came by made my skin crawl.

For years I recognized this people-worship thing where you're seen as a hater just cuz you want privacy.

Now I'm safe with a fence and no one knows I exist--but back then without protection I was hexed.

The more I avoided getting involved the more they'd send over "counselors" saying I didn't love God.

SOCIAL CHANGE WITH DEMOGRAPHIC SHIFTS

I'm a racist if I believe in immigration laws and a border. That's how crazy it is in this era.

If Hamas had no weapons there'd be peace. If Israel had no weapons they'd be DESTROYED.

It used to be about public service but now it's big bucks and post-service opportunities.

DONE. Stats show liberals block conservatives for their views--well now I've had it with you.

As the news rehashes the screw job over and over and we go under don't forget our Father.

These were the social expectations before the internet made us all independent of social group tyranny.

The whole white town was cruel but suddenly the demography changed with high school 99% Hispanic.

BY A THREAD

Suddenly the white boys weren't creating havoc in gangs cuz they were replaced by immigrants.

Suddenly the white boys weren't so hoity toity and arrogant, and simultaneously males were being belittled.

Suddenly the white boys weren't getting away with things and the cops put em away with set-up stings.

My tormenters are in their fifties with kids scattered here/there, probably don't remember the whole affair.

Once the demography of a town changes, everything changes. In my particular case I was saved by it.

Hoity toiti: snobbish, haughty, condescending, disdainful, patronizing, snobby, conceited, proud, arrogant.

Hoiti toiti 2: supercilious, superior, imperious, above oneself, self-important, overweening, lordly, lofty.

They see the refined as snooty, uppity, uppish, la-di-da.

What scares me about people is them thinking they own you then getting angry if you just wanna be alone.

Intellectual maturity is overcoming constraints. The immature mind just seeks to please the ranks.

MEDIA IS THE DEMOCRATIC PARTY

The media is an outlet for the democratic party and liberals will pay the price for this treachery.

Liberals living in gated communities saying those in poverty should have no police guarding.

White supremacists are the biggest problem we have in America today, beyond ISIS. J. Biden

BY A THREAD

Inciting racial division is the only way the democrats stay in power and we're sick of em.

When you hear the Star Spangled Banner they want you to think: oppression-- a dam lie son.

America became the envy of the world not thru self-loathing but in dedication to principals.

The way you succeed in America is thru diligence and self-discipline which they say is racism.

Stupid people shouldn't be ignored as if they're not a threat. Low IQ creates most violent.

KEYWORDS ARE VERY TELLING

If they say "inclusive" or "climate change" or "diversity" then you know they're dense dullards and shady.

They are so weak, terrified to go against the grain. It's not just loss of income, the liberal herd is mean.

I'm just happy I was able to complete the job God gave me to do. That's really the most important too.

Whether or not He rewards me, well I'm not thinking that way. Altho' I am anticipating it every day.

God said Double for your Trouble. He's doubled me on many things and also separated me from rabble.

They're so needy for approval, seeking to get it that way--but make fools of themselves by what they say.

You know climate change is all a scam but you go along with it in some way and it's an embarrassment ok?

Sexual impurity produces mental vacuity and that's why they look so empty.

BY A THREAD

The sinful underworld is so complexly developed they take it for granted as normal but it's BAD, all of it.

Homosexuality is wrong, bad, evil and dangerous. Schools/media telling you its superior is outrageous!

Lesbians! Yuk three times--you mean you do those things? That's what I think just like other earthlings.

I suppose I'll be censured/banned cuz I said homosexuality is evil. But it is and God hates it, read the bible.

MEN KISSING MEN, WOMEN KISSING WOMEN

A man kissing a man, are you kidding me? And stop your kissin' and huggin' women, I'm sick of thee.

My problems only came from contorting myself to fit people's expectations. But alone: mental explosion.

My German and Scotch ancestors lived on potatoes as a major staff and it'll be mine too, no reactions yet.

She got so used to being imposed upon she lost her soul and just went on, abused by daughter/son.

I'm watching you and I don't like what I see. One more trick, manipulation or lie then get away from me.

High taxes/regulations, open borders/aliens, trash and the homeless: this was beautiful California.

Stop saying "unity is the way". There's no way good can unite with evil, we must DIVIDE from it, ok?

There's been a gangsterization of the U.S. government as we fear the knock on the door at any moment.

DIET UPDATES

BY A THREAD

I felt ok on fruit and fat however the fat created false body tissue that is now receding on <10%fat.

The same foods causing disease cause acid reflux. That's something to chew on if you want that pain gone.

There's one junk food I love: Cheetos! But if I dare eat em I have acid reflux for 3 days so I say NO.

Yes I had a mental illness but it's all over now and that's all you need to know. It was genetic/social anyhow.

Eat like a peasant: fill up on beans, rice, corn or bread for breakfast and then in the aft, just juice.

As the story of Daniel portrays, if you eat like a peasant God'll make you a handsome rich man.

SMOOTHIES, SOUPS, STEWS

I love it and I miss it but lungs are wounded by it and the edibles make me psychotic/a twit.

"I vomited all the time and I don't know why". Honey in Who's Afraid of Virginia Wolf.

Oh God thank you for cheese. It's calorically dense so I don't need a lot to satiate/give energy.

If you cough after taking a toke you should never have smoked, that's what I finally found out.

Cheetos to celebrate, a three day fast to dissolve the block like concrete, not worth it see.

Old movies are like a time capsule, a magic transport. For those who are deep it's so therapeutic.

If you're with the right people, nothing need be said. They just know and that's a true friend.

BY A THREAD

How to view it: We swim in muddy waters, I was young and foolish, didn't know any better.

Make your work available and then whoever needs to see it will and you'll be at the finish.

It's the Negredo stage in making gold, feeling no one's as depraved as you. Let it cycle through.

RECAP ON THEIR EVIL MAP

When involved with a narcissist they must triangulate you--ever getting people against you.

They will distort the truth to fit their narrative and leave no stone unturned influencing relatives.

They put you on a pedestal then one slip up and out comes attacks from the unresolved self.

To learn all this on a gut level I had to endure incredible things but it's worth it for the wisdom.

Those who had the most to lose did the least to prevent its happening. Ronald Reagan.

God doesn't want you trapped with a jealous loser so open your mind & God pulls the trigger.

RECAP OF THE CREATIVE ACT

A Creative Act is an actual structure in nature. It comes through a person, that's the literature.

The Creative Act comes thru a strange person, an oddball from another world: potential victim.

Completion of the Creative Act comes from the strength to show the unique has class.

Let real life pull you away from the dam computer. Feel the sun, order drawers, cook, correspond.

THE TRADITIONS OF MEN VS. GOD

The traditions of men change constantly--why put faith in them? Don't get swept up friends.

The traditions of men are the basis of all false religion and they're everywhere--it's not Him.

Tho' the most famous philosopher ever, Nietzsche never got one review of his early works.

Nietzsche went mad upon entering the deep collective unconscious but I've already done that.

The strange bizarre customs of other people we're supposed to adapt to, re: animals too.

I won't be here when the Kalergi Plan comes to roost fully, but it will be communism honey.

When a cop helps the homeless you're told to think it's white supremacy--it's ridiculous see.

Man can't know his lowness, he takes what he sees as the only reality bashing you the highness.

Evolution of the left: They now hate white people, Jews and Asians--anyone who's achievin'.

PLOY: load up a bill with a ton of socialist policies and gov expansion calling it "infrastructure".

America should never apologize. It's far more important to be effective than woke. Matt Gaetz

The root cause of mass migration: Third World countries are not as nice as America.

BY A THREAD

LIES WE BUY/WHAT TO BUY

Not a buncha worthless accomplishments but digging deep in private then blooming in public.

Not embarrassing self-promotion but truly doing something then on you: a tiny biography.

Why be jealous of me unless you wanna do what I did, arise for work at midnight my entire life.

"When I maladapted to his resumption of drinking he was so tricky they turned against ME". Lady

Only two stored juices: V-8 juice all the vegetables and the superior antioxidant, pomegranate.

V-8 AND POM don't require refrigeration or cooking and they will keep you alive, maximally.

A little pomegranate or V-8 juice is not a meal but a snack. Store these in your closet.

With both the picturestrips and the music it's the CHANGES which evoke thought/insights.

TERSE VERSE

I know men and don't wanna impose on you sir so I developed the art of terse verse.

Tables have turned but why did they have to die out first? I literally had to outlive the curse

Of course old crones go into isolation in an ageist culture where cruel remarks are flyin'.

TABLES HAVE TURNED

Terse verse: GET IT IN before they have a chance to argue with it then they see truth finally.

Go ahead and write on your leftist narratives in long boring paragraphs, the right is concise.

I did it. I built my empire and that is that. It's all there for all to see, self-edify or for a laugh.

Misfit Soren Kierkegaard's tomb reads: Now I sleep in valley sweet, just with Jesus will I speak!

Just because she's clever doesn't mean she's devious. Don't fear her great smarts, use it.

FALSE EQUIVALENCIES

False equivalencies between true democracies [rule of law] and terrorists shows only prejudice.

False equivalencies give cover to terrorist groups while instantly discounting their arguments.

False equivalencies reveal prejudice and a weak argument: reject em now that you know it.

They attacked me for not saying "he and she" rather than just "he" and I lost all my creativity.

I'm whole now, mature. I'm the world card, I built an empire. But there was a time of war.

The Hero's Path is zigzag: Sick cycles of ups and downs, drastic changes moving upward.

Masculinity: Enforcing order in your community but brave and courageous when necessary.

The political parasite: pimping the pain of the people after creating divisions of good and evil.

As we mature and look back it's extremely embarrassing but forget it, we all have that.

100 KAREN KELLOCK BOOKS

AFFINITY OR MISERY
AGELESS CORNUCOPIA
AMERICA AWAKE!
AMERICA'S DAFT ERA
ARTS OF PALEO FASTING
AUTOPHAGY ON CHEATERS
BACKSTABBING NEUROTICS
BETRAYAL TRAUMA
BOOMERS AND BROKENNESS
BOOT ON NECK
CHAMPION GUIDES
COMMIE NUTHOUSE
COMMIES
COMMUNIST SPIRIT
CONTAGION OF MADNESS
CONTAGIOUS MADNESS
CULTURE CLASH BASHED
DAFT LEFT
DAILY FASTARIAN
DAM RATS
DIVERSITY IS CRUELTY
E-RACE WHITE
EVIL FREAKS (Beyond Gross)
THE END OR A BEND?
FEMALE BULLIES AND FEMI-NAZIS
FEMALE CARNALITY
FEMALE DUMB DOWN
FEMALE POWER DRIVE
FEMINISM AND RUIN 1 & 2
FIX FOR MISFITS
FOOLS & TRAMPS
FREEDOM SPEAKING
FRENEMY ENABLER
FRENEMY LIAR
FRENEMY THIEF
FRENEMY TRAITOR
TRENEMY TYRANT
GENIUS IS HELD DOWN
GLOBALISLAM
GOD USES THE FLAWED
HAZE OF THE LATTER DAYS

THE HERD IN WORDS
HIX POLITIX
HOW THEY RUINED US
JUST SKIP DINNER
LE FEMME AND THE COMMUNIST SPIRIT
LIBERAL CHAOS & ROT
LIBERAL DOUBLETHINK
LIBERAL GALL 1 & 2
LIBERAL SHOVE-DOWNS
LOCK YOUR GATE
LOSERS and Femme Fatales
MANUAL FOR SUPERIOR MEN
MODERN ART FROM HELL
MOSTLY FAKE
NOTES TO CHAMPS 1 & 2
OVERCOME FRENEMIES
PC MAKES US CRAZY
PEOPLE ARE CRUEL
PEOPLE PROBLEMS 1 & 2
PERSECUTED GENIUIS
POLI-PSYCH MYSTERIES
PRETENTIOUS SLOBS
QUEEN BEE
RED NEW DEAL
RETURNING TO FIRST NATURE
SEASON OF TREASON
SEPARATE MEANS HOLY
SOCIAL HYPNOTISM
SOLITUDE SOLUTION
SUPERCILIOUS
THE SCHOOLS SCREWED EM UP
TOAD TO PRINCE
TRIALS CYCLES
TRUMP VS. GROUP
TRUST IN TRASH
THE TRUTH ABOUT PEOPLE
UNDERHEANDEDLY CLEVER
WALK TALL WITHIN WALLS
WE'RE NOT ALL ONE
WINNERS SKIP DINNER
WORK OR SMERK

AUTHOR BIO
Karen Kellock Ph.D.

Ph.D Political Psychology, UCI 1976
Post-Doctoral: UCI Medical School
Department of Psychiatry
Grants NIMH, NIAAA

Ph.D. dissertation "A Systems-Theoretic View of Pathologic Interaction" made an early mark as the "Wife of the Alcoholic Syndrome". Postdoctoral research at UCI Medical, Dept. of Psychiatry on the systems surrounding pathology on NIMH and NIAAA federal grants: *The Contagion of Madness: The Psychology of Neurotic Interaction and Pathological Systems.* Therapy tool Therapeutic Playwriting introduced the play *Mary and Murv: Gruesome Twosomes in the Alcoholic Marriage.* She taught Abnormal Psychology and Pathological Systems Theory at UC and CSU campuses and developed "the Debris Theory of Disease" in five books and website: (www.karenkellock.org): *Champion Guides, Daily Fastarian, Just Skip Dinner, Arts of Paleo Fasting, Ageless Cornucopia. Manual for Superior Men is a* pick-it-up-anywhere book that you can't put down (20,000 Kellockialisms) and ever on your desktop it should be found (or this Ebook for superior wordsearch of new jargon).

www.ingramcontent.com/pod-product-compliance
Lightning Source LLC
Chambersburg PA
CBHW062045280526
45788CB00003B/1120